Islam from Scratch

Islam from Scratch

A GUIDE FOR NEW MUSLIMS

BRANDON RICHEY

in collaboration with
Islamic Society of Denton

TUGHRA
BOOKS

New Jersey

Published by Tughra Books

335 Clifton Ave., Clifton,

NJ, 07011, USA

www.tughrabooks.com

Library of Congress Cataloging-in-Publication Data

Names: Richey, Brandon, author.

Title: Islam from scratch : a guide for new Muslims / Brandon Richey, in collaboration with Islamic Society of Denton.

Description: Clifton : Tughra Books, 2021.

Identifiers: LCCN 2020047916 (print) | LCCN 2020047917 (ebook) | ISBN

9781597849432 (paperback) | ISBN 9781597849784 (ebook)

Subjects: LCSH: Islam--Handbooks, manuals, etc. | Islam--Customs and practices.

Classification: LCC BP174 .R53 2021 (print) | LCC BP174 (ebook) | DDC

297--dc23

LC record available at https://lccn.loc.gov/2020047916

LC ebook record available at https://lccn.loc.gov/2020047917

CONTENTS

How To Use This Guide

Welcome to Islam from Scratch, a handy piece of literature for new converts young or old, male or female, rich or poor. If you've been dipping your proverbial toe into the waters of Islam, you'll find the water is quite deep! There is an enormity of information, and that's where this book comes in.

The guide has been designed to feed you relevant information in parcels – each chapter acts as a milestone for you to complete before moving on to the next chapter, with a focus on helping you gather up skills and knowledge incrementally.

This book is not intended to be an authoritative guide on matters of Islamic fiqh, or jurisprudence. Rather, it's to help build a sense of comfort and understanding with what will feel like a very complex and simultaneously deep religious tradition. For any particular rulings regarding something you read here, consult an Imam or scholar for more nuance or information.

Each section is designed with minimum burden in mind, not to overload you with information. You will learn the essentials in segments, with more information following once you've demonstrated some mastery over what is expected of you.

What do we mean by "expected" of you?

There are two major components in Islamic practice - *fard* and *Sunnah*. *Fard* components are mandatory, things that are considered an obligation is Islam. There is no wiggle room for the need to perform these actions, but for newcomers there can be some confusion about the division between that which is *fard* and that which is *Sunnah*.

Sunnah components are the actions and words of the Prophet Muhammad ﷺ, and are considered commendable if followed. Many Muslims incorporate aspects of the Sunnah into their worship. Think of the Sunnah as extra credit – it is not necessary to mold your life to the Sunnah, but the benefits of doing so are numerous both in this world and in the next.

Further than that, there are levels of "permissibility" in Islam with regards to the things we do. Some are mandatory, some are prohibited, and some are simply recommended. Those are:

😊 **FARD** - Obligatory

🙂 **MUSTAHABB** - Recommended

😐 **MUBAH** - Allowed

🙁 **MAKROOH** - Disliked

☹️ **HARAM** - Forbidden

Whenever a major point is listed, it'll have its associated "rating" attached to it to give you an idea of its place in Islam, as well as its importance.

Each chapter will begin with a set of objectives, and at the tail end will have related videos, readings, new vocabulary terms, etc., for you to glean. Hopefully everything is designed in such a way to make assimilating information as easy as possible.

Finally, as with all things as large and complex as religious beliefs, there are differences of opinion about how to interpret things. This book is written from a Sunni Muslim perspective, but even within the Sunni tradition there are four major schools of thought: Hanafi, Maliki, Shafi'i, and Hanbali, which differ on mostly very minor issues.

Whenever giving any information I'll do my best to give the perspective that all Muslims agree on, and leave notes that there are differences of opinion beneath them. If something seems interesting to you, by all means look into it! There's a diversity of opinion about Islam's inner-workings, and I encourage everyone to investigate.

Chapter 1

What Does It Mean to Be Muslim?

Assalamu alaykum, brother or sister. If you are reading this you have likely taken your first steps as a new Muslim, and now share a connection with over 1.9 billion fellow believers across the world. We are an expansive *ummah*, or the Muslim community, and stretch from the west coast of the United States to the deserts of Saudi Arabia, to the mountains of Pakistan, and to the shores of Indonesia.

With that in mind, and with that level of diversification laid out, Islam is built upon fundamental tenants called the "Six Articles of Faith" FARD: ☺

1. The belief that there is only one God worthy of worship, and that is Allah.

2. The belief in all of the prophets of God, including Moses, Jesus, and the final messenger – Muhammad ﷺ (peace and blessing be upon him).

3. The belief in the angels, as perfect beings made of light. Apart from angels, Muslims also believe in other spiritual beings, like the jinn.

4. The belief in the existence of all of the Abrahamic scriptures – the Qur'an, the Gospel, the Torah, and the Psalms.

5. Belief in the Day of Judgement, as well as life after death.

6. Belief in the Divine Decree, and that nothing happens without Allah's permission.

It would be safe to say that this is the bedrock for the faith, and that to be considered a Muslim you would have to accept these as the truth.

If you are coming from an Abrahamic background, like Christianity or Judaism, then these probably sound pretty familiar already! Prophets, an afterlife, a singular God, holy scriptures, and angels.

For my formerly atheist or agnostic brothers or sisters, like myself, I imagine it's a lot to take in. We've all been skeptical of faith at one point in our lives; even true believers ask themselves "why?" on more than one occasion. I have some good news for you, though – Islam has answers, and encourages you to think deeply on these questions.

But what does it mean to be Muslim?

Islam gets a very bad reputation when it comes to public perception in the West, namely because it is widely misunderstood. I will freely admit that a lot of that comes from a lack of dialogue between Muslims and non-Muslims, and so it's my hope to lay out a framework for how faith affects our actions.

Firstly, the relationship between a Muslim and God is very personal. There are no intermediaries in the Islamic faith – God hears us all equally and accounts us all equally. You talk *directly* to Allah. The Qur'an states:

> "Indeed, it is We Who created humankind and fully know what their souls whisper to them, and We are closer to them than their jugular vein."

Al-Qaf 50:16

Another cornerstone of the Islamic faith is one of social justice. During the time of the Prophet Muhammad ﷺ there was a great deal of inequality between those in power and those without power. The status of women, minority groups, the poor, the orphans, the slaves, all of these groups were institutionally disenfranchised by the ruling class of Mecca.

Islam seeks to radically alter these social relationships in a way that elevated everyone to a status of equality. Women were granted rights that would be considered radical in the 7th century, and those less fortunate were to be given comfort, material, and financial assistance in order to help elevate their position in society. If anyone is found wanting, this was considered a fault on the part of the state and the community.

It is the duty of a Muslim to right wrongs where they see them – to stand up for those who cannot stand up for themselves; to give to charity and to the needy; to look after the rights of others; to respect their families; to have patience and kind words for others, and to not backbite. This was the decree of Allah in the holy Qur'an:

> "O you who believe! Be upholders and standard-bearers of justice, bearing witness to the truth for God's sake, even though it be against your own selves, or parents or kindred. Whether the person concerned be rich or poor, (bear in mind that) God is nearer to them (than you are and more concerned with their well-being). So do not (in expectation of some gain from the rich or out of misplaced compassion for the poor) follow your own desires lest you swerve from justice. If you distort (the truth) or decline (to bear truthful witness), then know that God is fully aware of all that you do."

> An-Nisa 4:135

Culture and religion – addressing negative stereotypes and false justification

As a convert, you've likely been seeing Islam referenced on television, in movies, in news segments, magazines, and newspapers. Chances are also likely that this coverage is unfavorable, especially if you live in a western country.

If you've ever heard Islam mentioned in the same breath as oppression of women, suicide bombings, honor killings, terrorism, or female genital mutilation then you should know first and foremost that these practices are **not Islamic**.

Islam celebrates peace, unity, justice for all, equality of the sexes, anti-racism, and a consciousness of Allah in all that we do. Anyone who performs any horrible act in the name of Islam is not acting on behalf of our *ummah* (the Muslim community). The reality of the situation is that people use Islam to justify their actions, but Islam does not grant them that justification.

It is heartbreaking that these things exist, but I would be remiss to not mention them. We live in an era where terrible things even in the most remote parts of the world can be found with the click of a button, and attempting to gloss over that which is widely publicized does us no favors.

It's also very important to mention that almost every Muslim-majority country has had some history of colonization by major western powers at some point in their history. With little room to develop on their own, the legacy of post-colonialism and military intervention has left behind huge power vacuums that less savory characters have happily filled to exert their own twisted forms of power. Do not let anyone cite these terrible people or factions as "representatives" of your religion – they are opportunists, nothing more.

The good, the bad, the haram – the Muslim lifestyle

As new Muslims, I think it's necessary to have a very frank discussion about the sorts of ethics that we follow. I'm sure there are some that you are already familiar with, but I'm going to start with the things that are considered **HARAM**, or impermissible, to a practicing Muslim:

1. *Shirk*, or creating any partners to Allah in terms of worship or status

2. Eating pork, or the meat of animals like dog, cat, monkey, etc., or any of their derivatives

3. Meat that has not been slaughtered in a manner deemed *halal*, which prescribes the blood to be drained and the animal blessed in the name of Allah

4. Intoxicants, including alcoholic and medicinal (unless either are prescribed by a physician for an illness)

5. *Zina*, or sexual relationship between unmarried people

6. Impermissible financial dealings, such as gambling or dealing in usury

Obviously, this list of do's and don'ts could be very extensive, because there are many things that could be considered impermissible within the *spirit* of Islam, but are perhaps not expressly forbidden in the Qur'an or the *Hadith*s (the sayings and actions of the Prophet ﷺ). For now, we're discussing the big, obvious ones.

Now time for a frank discussion regarding these things – **it is not necessary to change your lifestyle all at once**.

I will write that again, for the people in the back – **it is not necessary to change your lifestyle all at once**.

We have to be aware of the fact that changing one's eating, clothing, and other habits is not easy. It is important to be cautious and perhaps choose a gradual transition as opposed to abrupt departures which may be more than one can carry at once. This is in fact how certain things had been first sidelined and eventually forbidden in the course of the Qur'anic revelation, such as alcohol first being restricted and then later being forbidden.

Think of yourself as a new Muslim in the purest sense of the word, living a lifestyle completely different than those brothers and sisters who have been raised in Muslim households. Many of my Muslim companions hate even the smell of pork, for example, while bacon still makes my mouth water when I see it. Again, it's all in how we were raised, and honestly our more seasoned brothers and sisters have had a lifetime to hone these skills and practices.

Imagine someone starting a new weight-loss diet after years of eating fatty fast food. They want to improve, so they stop eating every unhealthy thing in sight and switch immediately to clean eating. What happens when you shock the body this way? It rebels, and eventually the mind will follow. They give up because it appears too hard, rather than making gradual changes to their diets until they are where they wanted to be.

How do you eat an elephant? One bite at a time.

Islam, for new Muslims, is a similar struggle. You need to reach a stage where all of these things deemed impermissible are no longer consumed, but it's going to take time before you can manage it with ease. Start very slowly, perhaps avoiding pork if you can help it and turning down alcoholic beverages when with friends.

To give you a personal anecdote, it took me a month to stop eating pork entirely and seven months to stop drinking alcohol. If you make an effort, Allah will make it easy for you. If your heart truly desires change, you will be rewarded for that effort in time. Do not beat yourself up for not adapting overnight to the Sharia's rulings, be patient with yourself and try to make these changes gradually, slowly, and daily.

With enough thought, practice, and mindfulness you will find all of these things second nature.

Chapter 2

Shahada, the Five Pillars of Islam, and Vocabulary

Goals in this chapter:

• Learn the importance of *Shahada,* and what makes for a valid *Shahada.*

• Know the Five Pillars of Islam and what they mean.

• Understand the six Articles of Faith of a Muslim's beliefs.

• Learn some basic Arabic vocabulary to better understand Islam and to better facilitate interaction with other Muslims.

Shahada FARD

A Muslim's spiritual and religious life formally begins by taking the *Shahada,* or the declaration of faith. It is one of the five pillars of Islam, but also something that forms the basis for our faith. So, what is it?

It is a simple statement of belief – there is no God but Allah, and Muhammad ﷺ is His messenger.

In order for the *Shahada* to be valid, you need to do only two things:

1. Have a pure intention of what you are doing; you must be under no coercion or obligation to say the *Shahada.*

2. Speak the words of the *Shahada* out loud, preferably in Arabic, certainly in your native tongue if you do not understand the Arabic. Those words are:

Ash-hadu an la ilaha ill-Allah,

I declare there is no god worthy of worship except Allah,

wa ash-hadu anna Muhammadan rasul Allah

and I declare that Muhammad is the Messenger of Allah.

And that's it. No big ceremonies, no tests, just a statement of faith and those nearby to see your testimony. From this point on you are a Muslim, and it is not the place of anyone to tell you otherwise. If you believe in your heart those words, you are one of the *ummah*.

The *Shahada* has a lot more relevance than simply becoming Muslim – we recite it when we pray, when we complete our *wudu*, and even out loud as a reminder of our beliefs every day. In a sense, the *Shahada* is our version of mindfulness.

The Five Pillars of Islam FARD ☻

Naturally if you've done any reading or research about Islam you will have found something called "the Five Pillars." Much in the way pillars hold a building upright, the Five Pillars hold up the religion of Islam. Without even one it would fall apart, and so it is prudent to think of these five things as highly important fundamentals of our religion.

Shahada – the profession of faith. As discussed in the previous section, the *Shahada* is simply the acknowledgement that there is only one God worthy of worship, and that Muhammad ﷺ is His final messenger.

Salah – prayer; more specifically the five obligatory prayers set at strict times of the day. We will cover *Salah* more in-depth in the upcoming chapters.

Zakat – almsgiving, or charity. A minimum amount of 2.5% of one's wealth is to be given to the needy, the stranded traveler, those in debt, or those who bring hearts together for Islam. This occurs once a year, and most popular during Ramadan. There is more to *Zakat* than just this number. For instance, *Zakat* becomes obligatory when a person's wealth reaches a minimum amount called the *nisab*. This is best discussed with a local Imam or scholar!

Sawm – fasting during the month of Ramadan. Every year we fast from dawn to sundown for the entire month, unless certain conditions prevent you from being able to fast. Prohibitions during fasting include eating, drinking, sex, and smoking. The entire concept behind the fast is to make you cognizant of those less fortunate than yourself, and to similarly recharge your faith and your devotion to the sick and the needy.

Hajj – the pilgrimage to Mecca. At least once during a Muslim's lifetime, if they are able, they should try to make the journey to Mecca. While certain factors can prevent a person from ever being able to make *Hajj* such as financial constraints or physical issues, it is strongly encouraged to complete this trip at least once. It is meant to follow in the footsteps of the Prophet ﷺ, and to also denote your devotion to Allah.

Each of these pillars needs an entire section on their own for the full details, but this is just a quick breakdown of their essence and anything important you may need to glean from a quick glance.

The two most important pillars to begin with are, of course, the *Shahada* and the *salah*. These are a new Muslim's first introduction to the faith, and set the foundations for how you will practice going forward.

If you have decided to join Islam during the month of Ramadan, well, I applaud your courage. You are the "summer courses at university" kind of Muslim, mashallah.

Vocabulary

Part of being Muslim means you are going to be exposed to Arabic and will have to learn some words. You will find that Arabic itself is submersed deeply in Islam and it is nigh impossible to separate the two, so let's start with some terms that will be handy for you going forward.

Arabic transliteration	English translation
Allah	The God
Qur'an	*lit.* The Recitation; holy book of Islam
Surah	Chapter of the Qur'an
Ayah	Verse of the Qur'an
Salah	Prayer

Du'a	Supplication
Adhan	Call to prayer
Masjid	Mosque
Imam	Leader
Fard	Mandatory
Sunnah	Sayings and actions of the Prophet ﷺ
Allahu akbar	God is the greatest
Assalaamu alaykum	Peace be unto you
Wa alaykum salaam	And unto you, peace
Bismillah	In the name of God
Al-hamdu lil-lah	Praise be to God
In sha Allah	If God wills it
Ma sha Allah	What Allah has willed

So, there is obviously a lot to unpack here; the table above is a handy guide for you to reference, but some of these things are going to require a bit more explanation. Let's break them down into their important parts!

Allah – the name of God in Arabic; the God with a capital G. More accurately translated as "the God," this is the same God shared with Christianity and Judaism. In fact, Christians that live in the Middle East (such as those Copts in Egypt) refer to God as Allah.

Qur'an – the Islamic holy book. This was revealed in verses and chapters to the Prophet ﷺ and was memorized and written down by his companions during his lifetime. After his passing, the Qur'an was codified by the successive leaders of the Muslim community (caliphs) of the day, resulting in the completed work that we have to this day. This book, unlike many other holy books of varying religions, is considered the literal word of God and has remained unchanged since it was first revealed.

Surah – a chapter of the Qur'an.

Ayah (Ayat, pl.) – a verse of the Qur'an, more specifically of a *surah*.

Salah – the obligatory prayers that must be observed at prescribed times of the day, and one of the Five Pillars of Islam. *Salah* is not simply prayer, but it is an entire ritual in and of itself. We will go into more detail about *salah* in the third milestone.

Du'a – a supplication, or "informal" method of prayer, *du'a* can be offered any time with or without wudhu. There are two types of *du'a* – those that you offer yourself based on your needs, and those that you offer for specific situations such as a *du'a* offered before traveling, sleeping, etc. We'll cover these more extensively later.

Adhan – the call to prayer at the mosque. A *muadhdhin* (the reciter) chants the call before each of the five daily prayers. While in Muslim countries the adhan is sung over loudspeakers and heard in the neighborhood, in other countries it is usually performed indoors. Much like the function of a church bell, the adhan is meant to notify Muslims that *salah* is about to begin. It is considered respectful to stop whatever you are doing while the adhan is being recited and repeat the words of the *muadhdhin*.

Masjid – the Arabic word for "mosque," you will often hear this word among Muslims more than the English word.

Imam – the spiritual leader of the masjid. The most American equivalent would be a priest or preacher for a church, though responsibilities differ depending on the masjid you attend.

Fard – the term is used to describe something that is obligatory, or compulsory, in the religion. For example, the five daily prayers are *fard* – mandatory. You cannot opt out of them, because to do so would be sinful and forgoing your obligation to Allah. That is not to say, however, that new Muslims need to act in a *fard* manner right out the gate – there is much to learn, and you will not be able to do everything at once. Take your time, practice your faith, and Allah will guide you.

Sunnah – the traditional customs and practices of the Prophet ﷺ that are encouraged, but not mandatory (when we talk about the Sunnah in this context, we are covering what scholars might call *nafl*, or extra credit. There are Sunnah practices that are mandatory, but colloquially we refer to the Sunnah as things that are good to emulate). *Sunnah* practices are based on the actions and sayings of the Prophet ﷺ, and thus have a lot of weight when determining a Muslim's actions. To act, speak, and pray in a manner that is close to the *Sunnah* is to bring yourself closer to Allah through the best example we have – His Messenger ﷺ.

Nawafil prayers – Also called *nafl*, *nawafil* prayers are the ones that are not obligatory, but are encouraged as optional extra deeds.

Allahu akbar – both Muslims and non-Muslims alike have heard this phrase uttered, most famously on television by images of Islamic radicals. Though it has a negative connotation among colloquial discourse in the West, the meaning couldn't be furthest from a harmful one – "God is great." We say it when glorifying Allah, we say it when we move in prayer, and we say it when someone is born, when someone passes, etc. It's versatile in the sense that Allah is always worthy of praise and remembrance, so let this expression nestle firmly on your tongue.

Assalamu alaykum – "peace be unto you." A greeting shared between Muslims when seeing one another and when parting company. If someone says this to you, always be sure to respond.

Wa alaykum salaam – said in response to "assalamu alaykum." These two expressions will be so built-in to how you interact with other Muslims that you might even forget you are doing it.

Bismillah – It means "in the name of God," and used when starting almost any activity. You say it to begin the act of *wudu*, when you start eating, when you start prayer, when you enter your home, and so on. It is a precursor to taking any action by seeking the blessing of Allah. When said with sincere intentions, Bismillah turns any worldly activity into an act of worship.

Al-hamdu lil-lah – almost a sort of inverse of *bismillah*, this means "praise be to God." You often say this at the end of any action, such as eating or drinking, but also as a way of expressing how you are doing. If you ask a Muslim, "How are you?" he or she may respond with, "Alhamdulillah." It's not necessarily a way of saying "I am well," since it doesn't denote a feeling, but rather no matter how well or poorly you may be feeling you thank Allah for the day.

In sha Allah – meaning "if God wills," this expression is used frequently in Muslim discourse. Whenever proclaiming you will do something, go somewhere, accomplish something, it is often good practice to seal that expression with *inshallah*. Even something as simple as, "I'll see you tomorrow, inshallah" is a way of denoting that nothing is possible without the will of Allah, and if He wills it to happen then it will happen; if not, then it won't.

Ma sha Allah – meaning "God has willed," it is the foil of *inshallah*. This is often used to express amazement or celebration, such as congratulating someone for accomplishing something or achieving a milestone in their life. It can even be used for something as simple as appreciation of the weather outside ("What a beautiful day, mashallah.")

These are all meant to help integrate you into the *lingua franca* of the Muslim world. While many Muslims are not native Arabic speakers, they nevertheless use Arabic terms when speaking to one another. You, of course, are no exception and should try and memorize these terms and their particular uses.

The best way to practice phrases is to simply talk to your fellow Muslims; you'll find that one trip to the masjid will result in a dozen utterances of "assalamu alaykum," followed shortly by "al-hamdulillah" when someone asks another how they're doing.

We'll re-use some of the nouns listed above in further sections, so don't be too hard-pressed to remember everything. Each according to their ability – this is not the last we've seen of Arabic!

Chapter 3

Wudu and Ghusl

Goals in this chapter:

• Learn what *wudu* is, and how to make a valid *wudu*.

• Learn what *ghusl* is, and how to perform *ghusl*.

• Know what renders a *wudu* or *ghusl* invalid, or breaks it.

A Muslim's relationship with water is interlocked with the practice of cleanliness. Even outside of preparing for prayer, Muslims use water to clean themselves after going to the restroom in an effort to remain free of even the smallest impurities. We use water to stay clean, to prepare for prayer, or to wash the dead before burial.

☻   *Wudu* **FARD**

Wudu is the process of rendering oneself clean from minor physical, or bodily, impurities before *salah*. Muslims will often do this many times a day, and it is a necessary prerequisite for prayer. Without *wudu*, there can be no *salah*.

What we'll do is break the *wudu* into two parts – the *fard* and *sunnah* of *wudu*. The parts that are *fard*, or obligatory, are explicit things you do not want to miss. These will be in bold, to emphasize their importance. The *sunnah* of *wudu* are those actions that you are encouraged to include, and from my personal experience every Muslim performs both the *fard* and the *sunnah* actions of *wudu* by default.

☻ 1. **FARD Make the intention, or *niyya*, to make *wudu* for the sake of Allah, and begin by saying *bismillah*.**

2. Wash both of your hands three times each, starting with the right hand, up to the wrist.

3. Take water into your right hand and use it to thoroughly rinse your mouth out, again three times.

4. Take water into your right hand and splash it into your nostrils, blowing the water out, three times.

5. **FARD** **Wash your face from the chin to the fore-** 😊 **head, and from the left ear to the right ear.** Do this three times.

6. **FARD** **Wash your arms from fingertips to elbow,** 😊 **leaving no part unwashed. How you accomplish this, either by running them under water or by cupping water into your hand and using that, is up to you.** Do this three times.

7. **FARD** **Simply wet your hands and run them** 😊 **through your hair from the top of the forehead to the back of the neck, and then back again to the forehead.** You do this only once.

8. Use your fingertips to clean out your ears while simultaneously rubbing the back of your ears with your thumbs, again only once.

9. **FARD** **Wash your feet with the ankle, either by** 😊 **placing them under running water or by cupping water into your hands and rubbing them until they are entirely wet and clean.** Do this three times.

NOTE: Some schools suggest that if you have a valid *wudu*, it is not necessary to take socks or shoes off again to renew your *wudu*. Simply wipe your hands over the tops of your shoes or socks, and your foot-washing portion of *wudu* is renewed.

These components that are considered obligatory were narrated in the Qur'an:

"O you who believe! When you intend to offer As-Salat (the prayer), wash your faces and your hands (forearms) up to the elbows, rub (by passing wet hands over) your heads, and (wash) your feet up to ankles."

Al-Ma'idah 5:6

The components that are *sunnah* in this case are the actions of the Prophet ﷺ, and it would be considered wise to incorporate them into your *wudu*. Allah wishes to make it easy for us, however, and if you find yourself in a position where you do not have ready access to water or the water is very inhospitable (perhaps ice-cold or boiling hot), then stick with what is *fard*.

Tayammum

There is another method of ritual purity one can perform if they have no access to water, and that is the *tayammum*. This involves using clean dirt to rub your hands and face with in the event that there is no clean water nearby. While rarely used to the point of many Muslims forgetting the name of this practice, it's nevertheless handy in a pinch if you find yourself in the wilderness somewhere but manage to deduce it's time to pray. We'll come back to *tayammum* another time, but I thought I might drop it off for daycare on this page in between *wudu* and *ghusl*.

What breaks your wudu?

There are a few things that break, or nullify, your *wudu*:

1. Passing any sort of bodily fluid or function (urine, feces, gas)

2. Losing consciousness (including falling asleep, but not if one nods off briefly while sitting or leaning against something)

3. Intoxication of any kind, either from drugs or alcohol

4. Sexual intercourse or discharge of any kind

5. For women, when the menstrual cycle begins

There are competing interpretations of what invalidates your *wudu*, such as if you bleed due to an illness, touching your private parts with your bare hands, or if you touch the opposite sex, even by shaking hands. But, for the newcomer, let's keep it to the universal interpretation.

Now that last point is very important, because sexual intercourse not only breaks *wudu* but also cannot be made clean with *wudu*. This is where *ghusl* comes in, and we're going to talk about that now!

Ghusl

This act of purification is something of a full-body cleanse of every impurity. However, this is the only method to cleanse someone of any kind of sexual discharge, from wet dreams to actual intercourse itself.

Just like *wudu*, there are components which are compulsory and which are optional – *fard* and *sunnah*. Again, I will bold the parts that are obligatory.

☺ 1. **FARD** **Make the intention to perform *ghusl*, and start by saying *bismillah*.**

2. Wash both hands three times, up to the wrist.

3. Wash the private parts with your left hand until clean, only once.

☺ 4. **FARD** **Rinse your mouth and nose with water, as during *wudu*.**

5. Wash your face three times with water.

6. Wash both arms up to the elbows, three times each.

7. Run your wet hands through your hair to the back of your scalp, and then back to the forehead.

8. Clean both of your ears and the back of your ears with your fingers and thumbs.

9. Let water flow over your head and down your body three times, ensuring that the root hairs are thoroughly drenched in the process.

10. Run water over the right side of your body three times, washing with your hands so that noth-

ing is left dry. Repeat this process for the left side of your body.

11. Wash both feet three times, ensuring you are not standing somewhere unclean.

12. FARD Ensure that water has washed your en- ☺ tire body, including places such as the armpits or the belly button.

13. Recite the *Shahada* when complete.

You'll notice the *fard* components are much sparser than the *sunnah* ones, and that is because the obligatory portions are mandated in the Qur'an while the optional ones are the actions of the Prophet ﷺ. The obligation comes from the Qur'an:

> "O you who believe! Do not come forward to (stand in) the Prayer while you are in (any sort of) a state of drunkenness until you know what you are saying, nor while you are in the state of ritual impurity (requiring the total ablution) save when you are on a journey (and then unable to bathe) until you have bathed (done the total ablution)."

> An-Nisa 4:43

When do we need to perform ghusl?

There are several reasons to perform *ghusl*, but outside of sexual intercourse they are irregular. It's safe to say that if you need to perform *ghusl* after any of these, then your *wudu* is invalid as well:

1. After sexual intercourse or ejaculation of any kind

2. Following menstruation for women

3. Irregular bleeding in women

4. Postpartum bleeding

Some advice regarding "hanging on" to your wudu

So there is going to be something that crosses every Muslim's mind at one point or another – that you might need to go to the bathroom or relieve yourself in some way, but you are "holding it in" in order to avoid having to make *wudu* again before the next prayer.

We're all guilty of this, and I'm no exception. However, I am here to give you a bit of advice regarding this – don't make yourself uncomfortable; it's MAKROOH.

There is a *hadith* narrated by Aisha where the Prophet ﷺ said:

> "There is no praying when a meal is presented, nor when one needs to relieve himself."

Muslim, 560

If you really have to go to the bathroom or have been holding in a fart for the last half hour, just take care of business and then make *wudu* again. The main reason for this is it distracts you from prayer when you are worried about the pain of the call of nature.

Helpful videos:

YouTube - "*Sunnah* Way to Perform *Wudu* (Ablution)" by WayofJannah

YouTube - "Ahkam in Brief - How to perform *Ghusl*" by ZT Media

YouTube - "How To Do *Ghusl* : Ritual Bath In Islam" by The Daily Reminder

New Arabic terms

Arabic transliteration	**English translation**
Niyya	Intention
Tayammum	Dry ablution
Wudu	Partial ablution
Ghusl	Full ablution

Chapter 4

Salah (Prayer)

Goals in this chapter:

• Learn the five daily prayers that Muslims pray every day.

• Learn what a *rakat* consists of.

• Learn to pray.

• Learn *surah al-Fatiha.*

• Learn to recite the *tashahhud.*

We've arrived at one of the most important aspects of Islam for any believer – the *salah*, or prayer. Around the world Muslims perform these five prayers every day at their prescribed times, and they are arguably one of the most important aspects of being Muslim. It is narrated in the *hadith* that the first thing Allah will ask us on the Day of Judgment after we pass from this world is prayer:

> "The first thing people will be accountable for on the Day of Judgment is Prayer. Allah will say to His angels (even though He already knows), "Look at My servants' Prayers. Were they complete or not?" If they are complete, they will be written as complete. If they are not complete, Allah will say, "See if My servant has Voluntary Prayers." If he has them, Allah will say, "Complete his Obligatory Prayer shortage with his Voluntary Prayers." Then the rest of his deeds will be dealt with in the same manner"

> Ahmad, Abu Dawud, and An-Nasa'i

Prayer has a lot of benefits spiritually, namely by being in contact with and remembering Allah. One of the key components of *salah* is that you stop everything you are doing and reconvene with your Creator, giving you both a connection and an appreciation for Him.

There are a lot of components to prayer that can really turn off a new Muslim. When you see other Muslims praying, performing bows and reciting long surahs in Arabic, you can feel like you need to really "catch up" to them. However, it's important to remember that you are still very young in this faith, and that you will need to crawl before you can walk.

Some advice for starting out

Before I put forward the large list of components of *salah*, I just want to pass on some good advice that was given to me by the immensely patient and kind Imam of our masjid – if nothing else, just learn the movements of prayer and recite: "*Allahu akbar.*" Allah is not obsessed with ritualistic perfection; what matters is what comes from the heart – if your intentions are pure and your desire to worship are at the forefront, suffice to say that is a better prayer than someone who nails each ritual but remains completely disconnected from Allah.

Another thing you might struggle with in the beginning is focusing on your prayer. You do have to remain tranquil and tuned-in when you pray, which can lead to our busy brains often straying away to other topics. While standing in prayer you might find yourself thinking about work, or the laundry, or your bills, or that one thing Karen said to you at the cafe that just really keeps bothering you because *you don't know my life, Karen!*

I digress. One way or another, you will need to practice something akin to what Buddhists call "mindfulness." *Salah* is a communing with our creator, praising Him and calling to Him. It's a moment where you are as close to Allah as you can get in this world, and you would do well to give Him your full attention.

One way you can do this is to focus on the words you are reciting. Often with Arabic as a non-native language, we can start to forget what the words mean. Focus on what you are saying, what it means, how that matters to you. Another way is to imagine something in front of you – perhaps the *Kaaba,* or a ray of light.

To be perfectly honest with you, as a new Muslim, I am still mastering this practice. I've gone most of my life without any real experience praying, and it's possible you have too! Be patient, discuss "strategies" with other Muslims, and every once in a while try and put yourself in a very focused headspace – perhaps setting up shop at the local masjid alone and giving Allah your full attention without distraction.

May Allah make it easy for all of us.

☺ *The five prayers – timing* FARD

So, Muslims pray five times a day, but do they do it all at once? Well, no – there are prescribed times for each prayer, and a prescribed number of *rakat*s, or units, for each prayer.

1. **Fajr** (dawn) – begins at dawn and ends at sunrise.

2. **Dhuhr** (midday) – when the sun passes its zenith, or when shadows are just beginning to show. Dhuhr ends when Asr begins.

3. **Asr** (afternoon) – when an object's shadow is the same length as the object, until the sun turns orange in the sky.

4. **Maghrib** (sunset) – from when the sun sets until the red light has left the sky.

5. **Isha** (night) – starts when the red light is gone from the sky, and lasts until the time before the Fajr prayer.

You might be asking yourself *how* you are supposed to deduce all of this as a modern human living in an age of precise times, GPS devices, and all that sort of business. Well, I've got great news for you – the expression "there's an app for that" plays just as much of a role here as it does for anything else, so naturally you can install *salah* timing apps on your phone to remind you of prayer times depending on where you are in the world.

These descriptors of shadow lengths and the colors of the sky are useful for a time without accurate time calculation, but these days we know exactly where the sun is in the sky at any given place in the world. There's no need to eyeball it, but if you ever *wanted to*, you could.

All of the prayers *except* for Fajr are valid until the next one begins. That means from the start of Dhuhr until the start of Asr, you can pray the Dhuhr prayer. Same for Asr, Maghrib, and Isha. The only exception to this rule is Fajr – that prayer cannot be offered after sunrise, which is only about an hour or so after the prayer begins. Yes folks, you will have to get out of bed early in the morning for this one.

Where did "how" we pray come from?

One thing you'll notice in the Qur'an is that it doesn't tell us *how* to pray, only when. This is where the *Hadiths* come into play – the Prophet ﷺ was instrumental in teaching the early Muslims how to pray properly.

> "Pray as you have seen me praying and when it is the time for the prayer one of you should pronounce the Adhan and the old-est of you should lead the prayer."

Al-Bukhari, 631

We're going to learn a ton about prayer as Muslims, as it is the bedrock of our relationship with Allah. For now, however, I intend to introduce it piece by piece.

Missing prayers

These prayers are *fard*, and it is considered a pretty

substantial lapse in faith to miss them. Islam puts a lot of emphasis on prayer, and it is important to try and make every prayer at the right time and not miss them.

That being said, if you oversleep or forget a prayer it is possible to make it up. It is narrated by Abu Qatadah that the Prophet ﷺ said, "There is no negligence when one sleeps, rather negligence is when one is awake. If any one of you forgets a prayer or sleeps and misses it, let him pray it when he remembers it" (Sunan an-Nasa'I 616). While this is good news for our heavy sleepers, it also shows that you cannot neglect your prayers while awake. If you skip one because you "can just do it later," that is intentionally missing out and therefore sinful behavior.

I understand it will be difficult starting out to adjust your lifestyle to match prayer. In a way, a prayer routine sets the tempo for your day. You will have to make some accommodations, but in time it will get easier. It took me many months to adjust my schedule around prayer, *especially* the Fajr prayer.

I am not, however, going to beat you over the head with this notion of having to make all five of your prayers the first year you are a Muslim. Again, you are starting from scratch, and it will take time to adjust. Be patient with yourself, and with the right intention Allah will make it easy.

I only advise that you consider keeping the prayer as the best form of obedience to Allah. If you take nothing else away from this guide, understand that the most important thing a Muslim can do is observing prayer.

☺ *Getting ready for salah* FARD

There are a few things you will need to keep in mind before offering your obligatory prayers:

1. You are in a state of purity, achieved through *wudu* or *ghusl*.

2. Your body is covered appropriately. For men, the minimum is from the navel down until passed the knees. For women, the entire body except for the hands, feet, and face.

3. The area you are praying, as well the clothes you are wearing, are neat and clean.

4. It is the appropriate time for *salah*.

5. You are facing the direction of the *Kaaba*, in the holy city of Mecca. This is known as "facing the *qibla*."

To make it easy for new Muslims when it comes to covering appropriately for prayer, I would recommend investing in some clothes meant specifically for the act. You can find religious clothing for a great price almost anywhere online, or perhaps at a specialty clothing store in your area.

However, if you can't find anything like that, then sweatpants and a long shirt will do the trick!

Just make sure that when you move the clothing does not ride up, exposing your lower back or your knees. Otherwise, what's the point?

Rakat – a unit of prayer

Prayer is divided up into different *rakat*s, or units. Each *rakat* contains a series of movements (standing, bowing, prostrating, sitting) and words being spoken. Each prayer has different numbers of *rakat* that must be completed to be considered fulfilled:

Fajr – 2 *rakat*s

Dhuhr – 4 *rakat*s

Asr – 4 *rakat*s

Maghrib – 3 *rakat*s

Isha – 4 *rakat*s

Salah

In this guide, prayer will be broken up into two components: the *fard* and the *sunnah* components. The *fard* is what is necessary to make your prayers complete, and the *sunnah* is what will enhance your prayers and will be something you should aim to fulfill when you are ready.

For this portion of the guide, I will list the **FARD** ☺ components as well as the *sunnah* components, which will be marked as **MUSTAHABB**. ☺

😊 **FARD** Make the intention to pray, aiming for the purpose of completing your prayer. Ensure you are facing the *qibla*.

FARD Making the opening *takbir*, or saying "*Allahu* 😊 *akbar*" after raising your hands to level with your ears.

1

😊 **FARD** *Qiyam*, or standing for prayer with your feet apart and your right arm resting over your left arm. How you accomplish this is debatable depending on the *Sunnah* – below the navel (1), above (2), or on the chest (3). All, however, are correct.

2

3

NOTE: If one cannot stand because of some physical limitation, then sit. If you cannot sit, then lie on your side.

FARD Begin by reciting, "*Audhu billahi min ash-shay-* *taan ar-rajim*" which translates to, "I seek refuge in Allah from the accursed Satan."

FARD While standing, recite *surah Al-Fatiha*, or the first surah of the Qur'an, beginning with *Bismillah, ir-Rahman ir-Raheem*. You will do this for every *rakat* of the prayer.

☻ **FARD** Say, "*Allahu akbar*." Lower yourself into *ruku*, or bowing down with your hands placed on your knees so you are at a 90° angle (women bend only slightly). Some schools of thought say you should raise your hands to your ears before starting the bow, like in the opening *takbir*.

MUSTAHABB While in the *ruku* position, recite "*Sub-* 😊
hana rabbi al Adheem" which means "Glorified is
my Lord, the Almighty."

😊 **FARD** Rise to *qiyam*, saying *"Allahu akbar."* Optionally, some schools believe you should lift your hands to your ears after bowing in *ruku*.

🙂 **MUSTAHABB** While rising, say *"Sami Allahu liman hamidah"* which means "Allah hears those who praise Him."

MUSTAHABB Follow this statement with *"Rabbana* 😊 *wa lakal hamd,"* which means "Our Lord, praise be to you" while you drop your hands back to your sides.

😊 **FARD** From *qiyam*, go down into *sujud*, or prostration on the ground.

To prostrate properly, your feet, knees, hands, and face should all be in contact with the ground and facing the *qibla*. This includes your nose and forehead. For men, your forearms, however, should remain off the ground and to your sides.

It is better if women rest their forearms on the ground and their body on top of their thighs.

MUSTAHABB While in sujud, recite the phrase "*Sub- hana Rabbiyal A'la*" which means "How perfect is my Lord, the most high."

😊 **FARD** Rise from *sujud* and sit on your knees, with your feet placed in a way that is comfortable.

😊 **MUSTAHABB** While in this position, recite "*Rabbighfirli, rabbighfirli*" which means "Lord, forgive me."

😊 **FARD** Return to *sujud* and prostrate yourself again.

😊 **FARD** If this is the first *rakat*, rise to your feet into *qiyam* to begin the second *rakat*.

FARD If it is the second *rakat*, return to sitting on 😊 your knees and recite the *tashahhud*. Once complete, rise from this position into the third *rakat* if the prayer has more than two *rakat*s.

FARD If this is the final *rakat*, return to sitting on 😊 your knees and remain sitting.

Once you have completed all of your *rakat*s, there are two components to close out the prayer.

😍 **FARD** On your final *rakat*, do not rise but remain sitting. Recite the *tashahhud*, or testimony of faith, after your prescribed *rakat*.

🙂 **MUSTAHABB** While reciting the *tashahhud*, whenever you recite "*Ashadu an la ilaha…*" point your index finger straight ahead until you complete it.

🙂 **MUSTAHABB** After reciting the *tashahhud*, recite the *Salat Ibrahimia*, or the Abrahamic Prayer.

FARD Turn to your right shoulder and say, "*Assal- 😊 amu alaikum wa rahmatullah*" (May the peace and mercy of Allah be with you), and then repeat on your left (called the *taslim*).

MUSTAHABB After prayer, it is recommended you 😊 remain sitting and seek the forgiveness of Allah, as well as make *du'a*.

And you're done!

Now, obviously we're going to need to explain a few components here – nothing is ever as simple as it may seem!

Takbir / Allahu akbar – the *takbir* is the opening for the prayer, reciting *"Allahu akbar"* to begin. Without the *takbir*, prayer cannot start.

Whenever you make a movement in prayer, going from *qiyam* to *ruku* or *qiyam* to *sujood*, you will say *"Allahu akbar."* Whenever you are being led in prayer by someone else, *"Allahu akbar"* is the call to move to the next portion of a *rakat*.

Surah al-Fatiha – reciting this surah is considered obligatory in Islam, cited numerous times in the *hadith* as a prime component. Now, to be honest with you, this is a big step for a new Muslim. We just got done covering Arabic terminology, but this is an entire chapter you have to memorize in Arabic and recite:

Bismillahi ar-Rahman ar-Raheem

In the name of Allah, the infinitely Compassionate and Merciful

Alhamdulillahi rabbil alamin

Praise be to God, Lord of all the worlds.

Ar-rahman ir-raheem

The most Compassionate, the most Merciful.

Maliki yawmid deen

Master of the Day of Judgment

Iyyaka na'budu wa iyyaka nastaeen

You alone do we worship, You alone do we ask

for help.

Ihdinas siraatal mustaqeem

Guide us to the straight path;

Siraatal ladheena an'amta alayhim,

the path of those upon whom You have bestowed
favor,

Ghayril magdoobi alayhim walad dalleen

not of those who have evoked anger or of those
who are astray.

***

Now, obviously we can't ask you to jump
straight into praying five times a day *and* reciting
entire Quranic verses from the get-go. There are a
few work-arounds, and then some fatherly advice
I was given on the topic.

Rather than reciting *al-Fatiha,* you can recite
the *tasbeeh, tahmeed,* and *tahleel* which consists of
the following phrases in Arabic respectively[1]:

Subhan Allah – Glory be to Allah

al-Hamdu lil-lah – All praise is due to Allah

La ilaha ill-Allah – There is no God but Allah

As for that fatherly advice? At the very least, simply recite "*Allahu akbar*" in prayer and do your very best. While you do this, however, work on your *al-Fatiha* with another experienced Muslim until you can comfortably recite the entire surah with ease.

Tashahhud – in this component of prayer you are praising Allah, sending peace to the Messenger ﷺ, the believers, and repeating the testimony of the *Shahada*. The entirety of it looks a bit like this:

At-tahiyyatu lillahi, was salawatu wattay yibatu

All the compliments are for Allah, and all prayers

and goodness

As-salamu alayka ayyuhan nabiyyu, wa rahmatullahi wa barakatu

Peace be upon you, O Prophet, and Allah's mercy and blessings

Assalamu alayna, wa ala ibadi llahis saliheen

Peace be upon us and upon the righteous slaves of Allah

Ashadu an la ilaha ill-Allah

I bear witness that there is none worthy of worship but Allah

Wa ashadhu anna Muhammadan abduhu wa rasulu.

And I bear witness that Muhammad is His slave and messenger.

***

This is just as long as al-Fatiha, you might be saying! You're right, it is a lot of Arabic to chuck at you all at once.

You are still learning, however, and naturally before moving on from this section it is important to learn and memorize the *tashahhud*. Of course, it will take time, so in the meantime you have a few options:

You can learn the English translation first, if that would be easier for you. Saying it in your native tongue is not prohibited until you learn the Arabic.

While you are learning the *tashahhud*, you can simply insert the *tasbeeh, tahmeed,* and *tahleel* that you used above in place of *al-Fatiha*.

Taslim – the *taslim* marks the end of the prayer. One cannot exit prayer without reciting it, just as one cannot begin prayer without the opening *takbir*.

In Islam it is believed that you have an angel on your right shoulder, cataloguing your good deeds, and an angel on the left shoulder cataloguing the bad deeds. When finishing prayer, you wish peace and blessing upon them both.

Further, it's also a way of wishing peace and blessings upon your fellow Muslims when in congregation. The *salam* is for the angels, but also for your brothers or sisters in prayer.

The Sunnah: Salat Ibrahimia – We went over some "extras" in the prayer, and one of them is the *Salat Ibrahimia*, or Abrahamic Prayer. This was narrated in Al-Bukhari, 3370, and goes as follows:

Allahumma salli 'ala Muhammadin,

O Allah! Send peace upon Muhammad

Wa ala ali Muhammad

And on the family of Muhammad

Kama sallayta 'ala Ibrahima

As you sent peace upon Ibrahim

Wa ala ali Ibrahim

And on the family of Ibrahim

Innaka hamidun majeed

You are the Most Praiseworthy, Most Glorious

Allahumma barik ala Muhammadin

O Allah! Please send blessings upon Muhammad,

Wa ala ali Muhammad

And on the family of Muhammad

Kama barakta ala Ibrahima,

As you sent blessings upon Ibrahim

Wa ala ali Ibrahim

And the family of Ibrahim

Innaka hamidun majeed.

You are the Most Praiseworthy, Most Glorious.

Perfecting your salah with time

This is going to take some practice, ladies and gentlemen. There is a reason children do not start learning to pray until they are 7 years old, and that's because it takes a long time to build up the both knowledge and presence.

Please be patient with yourselves! You will likely spend days and days simply reciting "*Allahu akbar*" in prayer, and that is completely fine. Much like how children are not held accountable for prayer because they do not have knowledge, we are not at fault for not having knowledge.

It is also important to make the effort to continue to improve. Do not put off learning the important components of a complete prayer – begin practicing and studying! The longer you wait, the more complacent you will become with regards to those *fard* components. Naturally we want you to succeed.

Recommendations for Arabic recitation and pronunciation

Whenever you are learning the Arabic for *surah al-Fatiha* and the *tashahhud*, it is best if you start by listening to it being recited and try to follow along, rather than attempting to follow by reading.

Arabic has a lot of tricky sounds that non-Arabic speakers may have difficulty visualizing in text format, so do your best to find a recitation either online or from someone in-person and attempt to mimic how they recite the *ayat*.

It is considered quite important to have a competent recitation of *al-Fatiha*. A poor recitation can distort the meaning, so do your very best to nail the correct pronunciation. I'll link some videos that will help you get started, but keep in mind that these often showcase **complete** prayers, including the *sunnah* aspects of prayer. Feel free to gloss over those segments for now, but if you want to start practicing a complete prayer then more power to you!

Helpful videos:

YouTube - "Learn Surah Al-Fatiha (The Opener)" by ServantOfCreator

YouTube - "Memorize Quran with ZAKY – Al-Fatiha" by One4Kids

YouTube - "My Prayer - Step by Step Guide to *Salah*" by Digital Mimbar

YouTube - "Reciting the Tashahhud" by SalafiTheTruth

YouTube - "How to Learn Tashahhud" by Islaah Media

YouTube - "How to Pray - (Description of Prayer)" by Islamic Center of TN

New Arabic terms

Arabic transliteration	English translation
Rakat	Unit of prayer
Qiyam	Standing up
Ruku	Bowing
Sujud	Prostration
Takbir	God is great
Tashahhud	Testimony of faith
Taslim	Salutations
Kaaba	*lit.* The Cube; the house of Allah in Mecca
Assalamu alaikum wa Rahmatullah	Peace and mercy of Allah upon you
Salat Ibrahimia	Abrahamic Prayer

CHAPTER 5

THE MASJID, PRAYING IN CONGREGATION, AND JUMU'AH

Goals in this chapter:

- Learn some new details about masjid etiquette.

- Learn how to pray in congregation.

- Learn about Jumu'ah, the obligatory Friday prayer.

When it comes to prayer in Islam, you've undoubtedly realized by now that it's exceedingly important. Doing it on your own is great to get into the habit of things, but it's even better when you do it in congregation. And where else to congregate with Muslims than your trusty local masjid?

Let's go to the masjid

If you have made it this far in the guide, I am assuming you have visited a masjid already. In fact, you probably took your *Shahada* there, too! Up until this point I wanted you to focus on just attending, visiting with your Muslim family, and praying along with them. There are a few "extra" tips I would like to arm you with, though, as you visit the masjid more and more:

1. Offering two *rakat*s when entering the prayer area. **MUSTAHABB**

It is *sunnah* to offer two *rakat*s when entering the masjid. This is called *tahiyyat al-masjid* ("greeting the masjid"), and it was narrated by al-Bukhari that the Prophet ﷺ said:

> "When one of you enters the mosque, let him not sit down until he has prayed two *rakat*s."

Al-Bukhari, 1167

This is getting into "*Sunnah* Prayer" territory, but I'd like to offer it up because it's good to get into the habit of praying two *rakat*s when visiting the masjid. You can do this by praying it the same as you do any two-*rakat* prayer, like Fajr!

2. If you see someone praying, don't walk directly in front of them. **HARAM** ☹

This is a pretty big breach of etiquette in the masjid. Imagine if a person praying has but a single string connecting them to Allah, and when you walk in front of it what you do is disrupt that connection. Regarding this the Prophet ﷺ says the following:

> "If the one who walks in front of a person who is praying knew (the sin) that is upon him, standing for forty would be better for him than passing in front of someone who is praying."

Al-Bukhari, 510

(It's is unclear if he meant forty days or years in this hadith.)

3. Always return a Muslim's "assalamu alaikum" with "wa alaikum assalam." **FARD** ☺

This probably seems weird to stick all the way down here, but it's actually considered **FARD**. ☺ You'll find even in the Qur'an, Allah states:

"When (whether traveling or at home, or in war or at peace) you are greeted with a greeting (of peace and goodwill), answer with one better, or (at least) with the same. Surely God keeps account of all things."

An-Nisa 4:86

You'll often find Muslims entering the prayer hall with a greeting, so be sure to return it even if they cannot hear you above everyone's response.

4. Learn to start dressing appropriately for visiting the masjid. MUSTAHABB

Ah, the dress code! Americans might know this as their "Sunday best," pertaining to visiting church. However, visiting a masjid is not all button-downs and dresses past the knees.

If you are new, don't sweat it too much. Most Muslims won't make it a habit to chide you on your dress, but *inshallah* they will encourage you to make better choices. I didn't own a single piece of culturally relevant clothing for eight months after converting, but I always made a point to wear pants and a long shirt!

Besides making your best effort to cover the body completely, it is MUSTAHABB for men and women to cover their heads; women with a *hijab*, and men with a cap such as a *kufi* or *taqiyah*. In different parts of the world this may or may not be a requirement (in some Muslim majority countries it is **FARD** to wear a head covering for both men and 😊 women).

As a revert, and likely one in a western country, just play it by ear! Be conscious, be thoughtful, and most importantly pay attention.

5. Network with other Muslims, especially those with patience.

One thing that is very crucial in developing as a new Muslim is making new friends within the community. Other Muslims help strengthen your *iman*, give you advice, answer questions, and keep you involved in the community. I would especially suggest seeking out other reverts who have also experienced this change in faith and lifestyle as you!

Get some phone numbers, email addresses, whatever you need to make a connection! Talk to your brothers and sisters, hang out regularly, make little groups to get together and discuss matters related to Islam. There is a wealth of information out there just waiting to be unearthed, and the more hands you have digging it up the easier of a time you will have!

Just make sure to differentiate between those Muslims that critique and those that criticize. Sometimes people have less patience for mistakes than others, so try and find someone who will be gentle with their support.

Praying in congregation

Ah, congregational prayer! This is what got me hooked on prayer in Islam before even becoming Muslim, and I hope it's as enjoyable for you, dear reader, as it is for me. You've likely followed an Imam in prayer by this point, so here are some things that you might not know about what the other Muslims are doing during prayer.

1. Never move before the Imam, or the one leading prayer, moves.

You never want to go ahead of the Imam in the moment; doing so is considered **MAKROOH**. If you can see who is leading the prayer, go along with his movements. If you can only hear him, wait until he says "Allahu akbar" before moving yourself. Make sure you do not lag behind – once he calls for a movement, you move, even if you are still completing al-Fatiha (Note: There is a difference of opinion whether one should recite al-Fatiha while praying with an Imam, or not).

For example, if you are standing and the one leading prayer is ready to move into the *ruku* position (and you cannot see him), wait until he says "*Allahu akbar*" and then make the move to *ruku*.

2. Always stand close to those next to you; close any gaps!

You've probably noticed by now that your personal bubble closes in rather quickly when you are at the masjid. This is because it's considered **FARD** 😊 to keep the rows tight and straight. The Prophet ﷺ said:

> "Straighten the rows, stand shoulder to shoulder and fill the gaps; be gentle with the hands of your brothers, and do not leave gaps for Satan. Whoever connects a row, Allah will connect him (with His mercy), and whoever breaks a row, Allah will cut him off (from His mercy)."

Abu Dawood, 666

You'll probably also notice that when a row in front of you has any gaps, people rush to fill them in. That is because it is important to always keep the rows ahead of you filled, so that the only row with available space is the rear-most one.

3. Not all prayers are recited aloud!

Something that was a headscratcher for me when I started praying in groups is that the Imam would not always recite during prayers. I found out later that the midday and afternoon prayers (Dhuhr and Asr) are silent. You recite them to yourself (or stay silent, depending on which school you follow), behind the Imam, while he leads everyone through the prayer with a simple "*Allahu akbar.*" Similarly, only the first two *rakat*s of the other three prayers are done aloud – any remaining *rakat*s are silent.

4. When reciting quietly, be sure you can hear your own voice. **FARD**

During these silent prayers, it is important that you be able to hear the words being spoken as you recite. It is narrated in the Qur'an, in Al-Isra:

> Say: "Call upon Him as Allah (God) or call upon Him as ar-Rahman (the All-Merciful). By whichever Name you call upon Him, to Him belong the All-Beautiful Names." And offer your Prayer neither in too loud a voice nor in a voice too low, but follow a middle course.
>
> Al-Isra 17:110

When praying quietly in congregation, make sure you are not so loud that you disturb those beside you. Nothing kills the mood more than trying to talk to God but hearing a hushed yet loud voice directly to your left or right.

Jumu'ah – what is it?

Jumu'ah (also called *jummah*) is the **FARD** congregational prayer that takes place on Friday, at the time of the normal Dhuhr prayer. For those of you familiar with Christianity, it is similar to Sunday services.

Jumu'ah is mentioned specifically in the Qur'an, in the aptly-named surah "Al-Jumu'ah."

> "O you who believe! When the call is made for the Prayer on Friday, then move promptly to the remembrance of God, and leave off business. This is better for you, if you but knew."

> Al-Jumu'ah, 62:9

What makes this particular event special is the inclusion of a *khutba*, or sermon, before the *salah* begins. Jumu'ah plays out something like this:

1. Adhan is called at the Dhuhr prayer time, like normal. This gives everyone about fifteen minutes to arrive, and then a second adhan is called to announce the start of the *khutba*.

2. The *khatib*, or person delivering the *khutba*, starts the sermon. Each sermon is broken up into two parts – the first part being the longest, and containing the bulk of the sermon.

3. The *khatib* sits down momentarily, and the second part of the *khutba* begins after he stands again. Normally this is a summary of the first part of the *khutba*, as well as a *du'a*.

4. The *iqama* is called at the conclusion of the *khutba*, signaling the start of *salah*. Rather than four *rakat*s as usual, only two are performed.

Jumu'ah is usually a great time to mingle with your fellow Muslims, since it is normally quite packed on these days. If you can manage to find yourself a "pack" that you go with every Friday, even better!

Attending Jumu'ah – who has to go?

☺ Jumu'ah is **FARD** for all able-bodied Muslim men, ☹ but **MUBAH** for women. The Prophet ﷺ said:

> "Jumu'ah is a duty that is required of every Muslim in congregation, except four: a slave, a woman, a child or one who is sick."

Abu Dawood, 1047

Men missing Jumu'ah is considered missing an obligation, especially since it is explicitly commanded in the Qur'an to attend. Missing three Jumu'ah in a row because of purposeful neglect is a big no-no.

But why are women exempt from Jumu'ah?

It is the wisdom of the Prophet ﷺ that saw the burden of managing a home meant that attending prayer would be a strain on the more family-oriented society of the early Muslim world. Women are certainly not barred from attending Jumu'ah, and may do so if they wish – women attended Jumu'ah prayer with the Prophet ﷺ and were not discouraged.

It is simply the agreed precedent that they are under no obligation to do so – only if they wish and are able. The alternative for women then, if they choose not to attend Jumu'ah, is to pray their Dhuhr prayer as normal at home.

Jumu'ah preparation and good practices

Preparation? You mean I have to prepare to go to Jumu'ah?!

Well, yes, but actually no.

1. There are some good practices to learn to make your Jumu'ah prayer more enjoyable and engaged, as well as practices that are considered *Sunnah*. ☺
MUSTAHABB

2. Take a *ghusl* shower beforehand, known as *Ghusl al-Jumu'ah*. This is the same as any other *ghusl*, but done specifically before the prayer on Friday.

3. Wear nice clothes to the masjid. This is a chance to spend quality time with Allah as well as your fellow Muslims, and it's good form to look presentable when you attend Jumu'ah.

4. Wear cologne/perfume when attending to give off a pleasant aroma when sitting in congregation.

5. Arrive early or on time to the prayer. It is said that the angels stand at the door taking note of who arrives on time, and once the *khutba* begins they depart to listen to it.

Read *Surah Al-Khaf* sometime between Thursday night and Friday midday, aiming to complete it. Recite the first and last ten verses to earn forgiveness and reward from Allah for your efforts.

Taking off from work for Jumu'ah

This is the tricky bit for a lot of us reverts. Since Jumu'ah is in the middle of a typical western work day, a lot of us need to find the ability to take a break from work or school to attend.

This can be especially compounded in difficulty if you don't want to let your boss, co-workers, or peers know you have converted to Islam. In countries like America, it can be a potentially uncomfortable conversation depending on where you work.

My advice is the same as all the other aspects of worship that you are working towards – **make the effort, but don't rush yourself into discomfort**. I did not attend my first Jumu'ah prayer until five months after I converted to Islam, and now I don't miss a single one.

If you desire a change, it will come; may Allah make it easy for you.

Helpful videos:

YouTube - This is What Happens Inside a Mosque... How to Visit a Mosque

YouTube - HOW TO GET READY FOR *JUM-MAH* (Friday Prayer) - Animated

YouTube - How To Attend a Muslim Friday Prayer Service (Jum'ah)

New Arabic terms

Arabic transliteration	English translation
tahiyyat al-masjid	greeting to the mosque
hijab	headscarf
kufi / taqiyah	rounded cap
khutba	sermon
khatib	narrator
iqama	second call to prayer
ghusl al-jumu'ah	Friday prayer ablution

Chapter 6

The Qur'an

Goals in this chapter:

• Understand the origins and history of the Qur'an.

• Learn etiquette with regard to how to treat a Qur'an.

• Learn about the importance of the Arabic language in the Qur'an.

The history of the Qur'an – the Word of God

The Qur'an has a very interesting history behind it, both in its revelation and in its development into the bound edition we have today. Unlike many voluminous religious texts, there is only one author: Allah; and it was delivered in only one language: the tongue of the Prophet ﷺ (Arabic).

For this reason, the Qur'an has been left unchanged since its codification, and its memorization and recital is done in the tongue it was revealed in. From the perspective of Muslims, to change any of these things would be to change what Allah has revealed for us.

Quranic surahs were revealed to the Prophet ﷺ over the course of his last 23 years. Rather than being revealed all at once, they would come bit by bit – usually following the need for guidance or after a big event. The *Sahaba*, or companions of the Prophet ﷺ, would transcribe the revelations on whatever was available at the time.

After the death of the Prophet ﷺ, the first caliph Abu Bakr was put into a position of tremendous responsibility when many of the Sahaba were killed at the Battle of Yamama. Their deaths meant that many who had memorized and recited the revelations were lost forever, and so the need to codify the Qur'an came to the forefront. The task was given to Zayd ibn Thabit, the primary scribe of the Prophet ﷺ.

> "So I started looking for the Holy Qur'an
> and collected it from (what was written
> on) palm-leaf stalks, thin white stones, and
> also from men who knew it by heart, un-
> til I found the last verse of Surat at-Tauba
> (repentance) with Abi Khuzaima al-Ansa-
> ri, and I did not find it with anybody other
> than him."

Al-Bukhari, 4986

The method for authenticating a surah from
the Qur'an was very thorough. It went as follows[2]:

1. Verses that were only memorized without proof
were not accepted.

2. The verse had to be written down in the presence of the Prophet ﷺ, out of fear the companion
had memorized it incorrectly.

3. If a verse was presented, two companions had to
attest to its validity.

After the collection of the Quranic surahs had
been completed, it remained in Abu Bakr's possession and then, after his death, the possession of his
successor caliph Umar.

However, by the time of the third caliph Uthman, the territory of Islam had grown substantial-
ly and the varying dialects of the Muslim converts
were beginning to affect the recitation across the
caliphate.

"Uthman then ordered Zayd bin Thabit, Abdullah bin AzZubair, Sa'id bin Al-As and Abdur Rahman bin Harith bin Hisham to rewrite the manuscripts in perfect copies. Uthman said to the three Quraishi men, 'In case you disagree with Zayd bin Thabit on any point in the Qur'an, then write it in the dialect of Quraish, the Qur'an was revealed in their tongue.' They did so, and when they had written many copies, Uthman returned the original manuscripts to Hafsa. Uthman sent to every Muslim province one copy of what they had copied, and ordered that all the other Qur'anic materials, whether written in fragmentary manuscripts or whole copies, be burnt."

Al-Bukhari, 4987

This act canonized the Qur'an we have today, rendering it unchanging and uniform. In only 20 years after the death of the Prophet ﷺ, the word of Allah had been preserved. We have the luxury of reading the Qur'an as the Messenger of Allah ﷺ and his companions recited it; an incredible concept!

How to handle a Qur'an

As the Qur'an is considered the word of Allah, its treatment should be done with the utmost respect. A few major points relate to how to handle a Qur'an:

1. Do not place it directly on the floor, and if possible do not stack anything on top of it.

2. Do not handle a Qur'an unless you are in a state of purity, such as one obtained after *wudu* or *ghusl*.

NOTE: There is some opinion on what is meant by "purity" in this case, since it could refer to the purity of the believers, but the four schools of fiqh clearly agree that *wudu* is **FARD** for handling a 😊 Qur'an.[3]

3. When reciting the Qur'an, begin by saying the *Basmala* (The first line from Al-Fatiha: "Bismillah, ar-Rahman ir-Raheem")

4. Read it slowly and with intention in order to absorb its meaning and to not regard it with haste.

5. Do not let a day go by in which you do not open it and look upon its pages.

These are just a few things, but enough to get you started!

Why Arabic?

You are probably wondering why it is so important to pick up the Arabic needed to read and recite the Qur'an, rather than your native tongue. Of course reciting it as you know your language is better than not at all, but efforts should be made to learn Arabic with time.

The Qur'an was revealed in Arabic, and thus because the language itself carries the word of Allah it cannot truly be changed, lest it lose some of its meaning. Indeed, it is why the English translations of the Qur'an are numerous and differ slightly – the Arabic language is rich in sound and meaning. To imagine that we are reciting the Qur'an in the same ways as the Prophet ﷺ should give us all cause for reflection and appreciation of the legacy being handed down to us; *subhanallah!*

Like most things in this book, I would like to stress that these accomplishments will take a lot of time to achieve. Many people already struggle with second languages, and Arabic is very different from most Western languages!

But Rome was not built in a day, and acquiring a difficult and very old language to read the word of Allah will require concerted effort over a long period of time. In this case, it is wise to find someone to help teach you and walk you through, step by step, the knowledge needed to acquire the language and recite it beautifully.

May Allah make it easy for you!

So, what should I do?

This is perhaps the tallest order of becoming a new Muslim – learning to read and recite Arabic. That being said, the Qur'an is a very important part of a Muslim's life and deserves a lot of consideration and attention.

If you find you are quite busy, read the Qur'an in your native tongue. Find the best translation for your language (for English we, meaning our masjid, generally recommend the Oxford World's Classics edition by M. A. S. Abdel Haleem), and read even just a few *ayat* a day. For Qur'anic commentaries to help you better understand it, something like "The Meaning of the Holy Qur'an in Today's English: Extended Study Edition" by Yahiya Emerick, or "The Study Qur'an: A New Translation & Commentary" by Seyyed Hossein Nasr, or The Qur'an with Annotated Interpretation in Modern English by Ali Unal, could be useful. Some Qur'an is better than no Qur'an!

Once you are comfortable reading in your native tongue, take some time to memorize some surahs that you appreciate. The most popular ones for memorization are the final three surahs of the Qur'an - Al-Ikhlas, Al-Falaq, and An-Nas. They are short, melodic, and make great accompaniment during prayer.

Helpful videos:

YouTube – "Learn Surat Al 'Ikhlas" by LearnEasyQuran

YouTube – "Learn Surat Al Falaq" by LearnEasyQuran

YouTube – "Learn Surat An-Nas" by LearnEasyQuran

Allah's Word – "Quran Audio with English Translation" – https://www.allahsword.com/quran_with_english.html

Soundcloud – "The Entire Holy Quran with 114 Chapters with English Translation" – https://soundcloud.com/submit2islam/sets/al-quran-with-english-audio

The Chosen One – "Al Quran with English (Saheeh International) Translation" – https://thechosenone.info/al-quran-with-english-translation/

CHAPTER 7

RAMADAN

Goals in this chapter:

• Understand what Ramadan is, and why it is important.

• Know the various rituals surrounding Ramadan.

• Know what constitutes a fast, what breaks a fast, and reasons to break a fast.

What is Ramadan?

You probably remember seeing Ramadan mentioned in Chapter 1 of this guide under the section regarding the Five Pillars of Islam. *Sawm* is this pillar, and Ramadan is the month in which we practice it.

Ramadan is the holiest month of the Islamic lunar calendar, marked to commemorate the revelation sent to the Prophet ﷺ in the form of the Qur'an.

During Ramadan, Muslims abstain from eating, drinking, immoral behavior, or sexual activity during daylight hours (the time between Fajr and Maghrib prayers). And for those who ask, yes – that includes water!

So, why do we fast?

For those new to fasting, it can seem perhaps a tad strange that depriving yourself of food or water would bring any sort of enlightenment. However, whenever you are hungry and thirsty you are very much *aware* of not only what is going on around you, but inside you as well.

The purpose of the fast is two-fold:

1. Greater appreciation and understanding for those who are less fortunate. Not everyone has access to food or clean water whenever they wish, and to willingly forgo it brings us closer to the

plight of those in need; it builds empathy and character, and hopefully a willingness to help alleviate the circumstances of the poor worldwide.

2. To increase consciousness of Allah, also known as *taqwa*. Because Ramadan is a time of spiritual reflection, improvement, and restraint, we are encouraged to be more aware of the powerful and encompassing nature of Allah.

Both of these actions are meant to improve the character, spiritual health, and wellness of those who practice it. Indeed, charitable donations during Ramadan are enormous and widespread.

Spending time praying at the masjid in congregation is greatly encouraged, especially for the post-Isha prayer activity of *taraweeh*, where one *juz'*, or 1/30th, of the Qur'an (about twenty pages) is recited each day for the full thirty days in an attempt to perform a complete recitation of the Qur'an.

To put it bluntly, Ramadan is normal worship on steroids – more prayers, more Quranic recitation, and a greater reflection of the relationship between the Creator and the creation.

Who has to fast?

Fasting is something only expected of able-bodied Muslims during Ramadan. Exceptions are made for:

1. The sick

2. Pregnant or nursing women

3. Elderly who would be hurt by fasting

4. Travelers

5. Pre-pubescent children

6. Women experiencing their cycle and post natal

If you become ill suddenly during the day after intending to fast, do yourself a favor and take food and water. You can make up the fast later!

What does fasting look like?

On the surface, fasting is abstinence from food and drink during daylight hours. However, it's a bit more nuanced than that:

😊 1. **FARD** Not ingesting anything through the mouth, food, medicine, or otherwise.

😊 2. **FARD** Not drinking anything, including water or medicine.

😊 3. **FARD** Abstaining from sexual intercourse with your spouse during fasting times.

😊 4. **FARD** Abstaining from smoking.

> "It is made lawful for you to go in to your wives on the night of the Fast. ... So now,

associate in intimacy with them and seek what God has ordained for you. And (you are permitted to) eat and drink until you discern the white streak of dawn against the blackness of night; then observe the Fast until night sets in."

Al-Baqarah, 2:187

So now we're approaching the idea of breaking one's fast, which we'll cover!

How is a fast broken?

This is a subject of nuance for a lot of Muslims, because accidents happen and those accidents may or may not break a fast. Here are some hard and fast rules for what breaks a fast:

1. Eating or drinking knowingly

2. Intercourse

3. Masturbation

4. Menstruation

5. Telling lies about Allah or His Messenger ﷺ

6. Inhaling smoke deliberately

7. Vomiting deliberately

Some of this is pretty clear, but you'll notice that eating or drinking *knowingly* is a qualifier. If you eat or drink something accidentally, unknowingly, it does not break the fast. This act is considered a gift from Allah, to provide you with nourishment while you are forgetful. This beautiful rule is narrated in a *hadith*, where the Prophet ﷺ said:

> "Whoever forgets he is fasting and eats or drinks, let him complete his fast for it is Allah Who has fed him and given him to drink."

Al-Bukhari, 6669; Muslim, 1155

What if I miss a fast?

There are two types of missed fasts – deliberate and unintentional. We'll cover the ones that are unintentional first, either by sudden sickness or menstruation.

If you *unintentionally* miss a fast, you can simply make it up another day after Ramadan ends except for those days on which fasting is prohibited (*Eid* being one of them). That was easy!

Similarly, if you are unable to fast at all due to old age or an illness which is chronic, you simply need to pay what is called the *fidya*, or feeding one person in need for each day of Ramadan. This amount can vary depending on where you live, but there are many organizations that will put together packages for those in need at a fair price either domestically or overseas.

If you *intentionally* miss a fast, however, it gets a lot more tricky and severe.

Doing this is considered a major sin, and an atonement is due for it (called a *kaffarah*). This can be accomplished by either:

1. Fasting two lunar months for each day missed

2. Feed 60 of those in need for each day missed

There is also some debate on deliberately missing a fast for things that are outside of your control; an emergency situation for example that requires you to eat or drink. For the more nuanced details about fasting, consult with your Imam or a scholar for details.

So, what does Ramadan look like?

Okay, now that we've gotten all those rules and guidelines out of the way, let's talk about something more fun! Actually participating in Ramadan.

If you are reading this you are most likely going to experience Ramadan from a western perspective, which can be kind of a bummer because Ramadan in Muslim-majority countries is a pretty big deal! Work hours change, restaurants are open all night, sleep schedules shift, it's a whole thing!

The Ramadan schedule

1. *Suhoor / Sehri* **MUSTAHABB** – this is the start of the ☺ day; the meal before the Fajr prayer. Typically you

will want to rise before the prayer time starts by maybe 30 minutes or so to ensure you get some food and water before the adhan. While highly recommended, it is not compulsory to have a suhoor early in the morning. However, there is *Hadith* literature to support it:

> "The Prophet said, 'Take suhoor, as there is a blessing in it.'"

> Al-Bukhari, 146

☺ 2. *Fajr Adhan (Fast Begins)* **FARD** – once you hear the call to prayer for the Fajr prayer, all eating, drinking, and smoking ceases. From this point on, the fast begins.

☺ 3. *Maghrib Adhan (Fast Ends)* **FARD** – fasting time is over! It's time to break the fast, often with an odd number of date palm fruits (1 or 3) and some water. Once the fast is broken, it is time to pray the Maghrib prayer and move on to what 1.5 billion Muslims around the world have been looking forward to.

☺ 4. *Iftar* **MUSTAHABB** – this is the meal eaten after breaking the fast, and is a big deal during Ramadan! If eating at home, it is customary to make food for your friends or neighbors and share in the celebration with them. Whenever visiting a masjid or community center you will often find an iftar feast waiting for you after the adhan is called!

Laylat al-Qadr

Translated as "the night of decree" or "night of power," this is considered one of the holiest days of the year. On this night the first revelation came to the Prophet ﷺ! The specific date, however, is a bit trickier than that.

Sunnis typically believe it falls on the night before the 27th day of Ramadan, but the certainty is unknown. Since it is believed to be somewhere during the odd dates of the last ten days, Muslims can worship on any of those odd days of Ramadan (the 21st, 23rd, 25th, 27th, or 29th).

This holy night is observed with prayer and supplication all during the night. It is believed that Allah delivers His mercy and blessing in abundance, prayers are answered, and sins are forgiven. Laylat al-Qadr has its own chapter in the Qur'an:

> Indeed, We sent the Qur'an down during the Night of Decree. And what can make you know what is the Night of Decree? The Night of Decree is better than a thousand months. The angels and the Spirit descend therein by permission of their Lord for every matter. Peace it is until the emergence of dawn.

Al-Qadr 97:1-5

If you get a chance to observe Laylat al-Qadr in the masjid, I encourage you to take it. It can be a truly spiritually-enriching experience.

The end of Ramadan

So, you've got the know-how to complete a journey through Ramadan, and you've reached the end!

The official "end" of the month comes when the new moon is sighted, which can cause some confusion between countries. If one country spots the moon but another does not, it does not necessarily mean Ramadan has ended. However, to play it safe, go by what your local masjid is going by.

The ending of Ramadan is marked by *Eid al-Fitr*, or "Festival of Breaking the Fast." This is considered one of two large celebrations to Muslims, with this particular Eid lasting three days!

If you thought the communal nature of Ramadan was evident throughout the month, Eid al-Fitr really ramps it up! Here gifts are exchanged, children are given money by relatives (called *eidi*), and visits to friends and family both living and passed are frequent. Think of it like Christmas Day, where family and gifts are a big tradition.

The end of Ramadan is a very bittersweet moment for many Muslims. While we are all relieved that we can eat and drink on regular schedules again, the spiritual and human connection we develop during this month cannot be overstated. The goal is to carry this newfound appreciation for faith and humanity forward into the rest of the year, and inshallah you will be able to! May Allah make it easy for all of us.

Helpful videos:

YouTube – "Ramadan, the Month of Qur'an by Mufti Ismail Menk" by One Islam Productions

YouTube – "What is Ramadan?" by How Deen

New Arabic terms

Arabic transliteration	English translation
taqwa	God-consciousness
taraweeh	Ramadan prayers after isha prayer
juz'	one of the 30 "parts" of the Qur'an
fidya	compensation for being unable to fast in Ramadan
kaffarah	compensation for skipping a Ramadan fast purposefully
suhoor	pre-Fajr meal in Ramadan
iftar	post-Maghrib meal in Ramadan
Eid al-Fitr	Festival of Breaking the Fast
eidi	gift

CHAPTER 8

BONUS TIPS, ADVICE, AND GROWTH

Welcome to the end of the book! You've come a long way, and I am very happy that you've read this far along. Inshallah, you are now well-versed in the fundamentals of Islam and how best to get started.

This is not an exhaustive text, as I said, and this guide should act as a springboard for you to seek knowledge and guidance on your own! The Qur'an states:

> "And these examples We present to the people, but none will understand them except those of knowledge."

> Al-'Ankabut 29:43

And the *hadith*s pile on the blessings:

"I heard the Messenger of Allah (ﷺ) say: If anyone travels on a road in search of knowledge, Allah will cause him to travel on one of the roads of Paradise. The angels will lower their wings in their great pleasure with one who seeks knowledge, the inhabitants of the heavens and the Earth and the fish in the deep waters will ask forgiveness for the learned man. The superiority of the learned man over the devout is like that of the moon, on the night when it is full, over the rest of the stars. The learned are the heirs of the Prophets, and the Prophets leave neither dinar nor dirham, leaving only knowledge, and he who takes it takes an abundant portion."

Abu Dawud, 3641

Knowledge is power, as the old saying goes, and Islam appreciates those who seek to educate themselves on the intricacies and otherwise. Ask questions, seek information, and always be willing to listen and learn. Further, never take one person's word for something – always look for a source!

For the sisters – to veil or not to veil

I've avoided talking about the hijab or any of the other choices of covering for most of the book, mainly because I wanted you to become familiar with the fundamentals of faith. However, I'd be remiss not to mention the act of covering oneself in Islam.

Yes, the Qur'an does call for women to cover their bodies modestly, which does include the veiling of the head.

However!

As with all things Islamic, there is no compulsion in religion. The desire to wear a veil to cover yourself should be a personal decision that you make. Allah has ordained what is best for us, evident in the Qur'an. If you decide that you want to honor Allah by choosing to wear the veil, then it should be a decision you make on your own.

I say that because often being compelled to cover through peer pressure or command by other Muslims can leave a very bad taste in one's mouth regarding the veil and its purpose. A veil does not equate with faith – a Muslim woman who covers is not necessarily more faithful than one who does not.

Take things as you deem appropriate and comfortable – you should desire to wear the veil, not feel compelled to do it. Allah will help you make the right choice when the time is right for you.

For the brothers – beard, or no beard?

I see this topic mentioned a lot by new Muslims, and even among lifelong Muslims – is the beard for men FARD or not?

There is no explicit obligation mentioned in the Qur'an regarding the beard. The evidence for this decision to grow the beard comes from the *hadith*s, where not only did the Prophet ﷺ himself have a beard, but had this to say about it:

> "Narrated Ibn 'Umar: Allah's Apostle (ﷺ) said, 'Trim the moustaches short and grow the beard.'"

Al-Bukhari, 781

The topic of beards being required or not is hotly debated between varying schools of thought. While some will say it is a requirement, there is no universal commandment regarding growing a beard. It can safely be called a *sunnah* however, and thus **MUSTAHABB**.

Personally, brothers should approach growing a beard in the way that sisters approach wearing hijab. If you decide to do it to better imitate the life and message of the Prophet ﷺ, then Allah will reward you for that effort.

Again, I will reiterate that a beard does not make one more or less pious. I am making an attempt to pre-empt any comments you might hear from other Muslims about how you *must* have a beard in order to be a good, practicing Muslim. To that, I say no – there are plenty of people who hide behind the outward appearance of piety to be monsters in private, and nothing you do should be done to please people – they should be done only to please Allah.

Moving away from intoxicants

The journey to quitting things like alcohol and marijuana is probably one of the toughest for reverts. Things like drinking are so ubiquitous with life in the West – when you have a party, a birthday, a celebration, or even just meet with friends, alcohol is typically involved. It's hard to say no, but I caution my brothers and sisters to take a slow and measured response to this.

In my experience, I've very rarely been happy about drinking alcohol after the fact; but I have been very unhappy with the results of drinking, either through the things I did while under the influence or the things that I said. When the Qur'an spoke about this mixture of the small gains vs. the larger costs, it fit right in with my experience:

> "They ask you about intoxicating drinks and games of chance. Say: 'In both there is great evil, though some use for people, but their evil is greater than their usefulness.'"

Al-Baqarah 2:219

I'll freely admit that there were times that while drinking I was more friendly, or generous, or compassionate. It does generate a high in small doses, but the great sin comes when we can't juggle the line between normal and excess. Human beings typically are horrible at self-regulation in life's pleasures, alcohol being a chief example among them.

I don't think I need to lecture anyone about the dangers of alcohol – there is enough research and plenty of concerned parents out there to tell us about drunk driving, liver problems, cancer, and so on.

The spiritual cost, however, is one you might not think of – forgetting Allah. Earlier in the book we talked about *taqwa*, and the remembrance of Allah in action and in prayer. While your mind is cloudy and hazy, we often forget Him while drowning in self-pleasure – missing prayers chiefly among those examples.

All things in Islam begin with intention though – intention to do the right thing, intention to make a change, intention to work for the benefit of others in the name of Allah. If you make the intention to quit drinking, sincerely, Allah will make it easy for you. It might not be that day, that month, or even that year. However, every time you make a sincere effort to stop it will become easier and easier to stop.

And with that sincerity comes a desire that you won't harm yourself for not succeeding every time you deign to stop. Trying, failing, and feeling remorseful for not succeeding are still worthy of praise, because remorse means that there is room for improvement and that you desire that improvement. When you feel nothing for doing something wrong, there is room to worry.

Lastly, I will say that overcoming the sins of addiction to the harmful things in this world will require a steadfast belief that Allah truly is *ar-Rahman, ar-Rahim* – the Most Gracious, the Most Merciful. If you desire the best for yourself, the best for what Allah has prescribed for you, and the best for that relationship then you need to remember His forgiveness every moment you can. It is narrated in the Qur'an:

> "And despair not of Allah's mercy; surely none despairs of Allah's mercy except the unbelieving people."

> Yusuf 12:87

I will give you a personal example of this struggle, just so you can see where I am coming from.

I struggled with alcohol before reverting to Islam. I was not quite an alcoholic, but I did drink in large quantities (my map tracker logged I had visited the liquor store almost 100 times in a year). Converting to Islam meant I had to start making changes, but this seemed impossible.

I continued to drink, making assurances to myself that I would quit at some point. However, it did not cease for months – sometimes it felt like I was trapped. Then, Ramadan arrived in the month of May and I promised I would not drink during this most holy of months. I begged Allah to take the desire for drink away from me.

And the funniest things happened – when Ramadan ended and I had been clean for the entire month, I tried to drink again afterwards to "reward" myself for my abstinence, and I found that I did not enjoy it at all. My desire for this was stripped away, and I have found myself much happier for it to this day.

It started with making the right intention, and while I did not get the results I desired right away I was rewarded for my persistence and my want for a better self.

May Allah make it easy for all of us.

Building a community

For a new Muslim it's very important to become involved in the Islamic community wherever you can find it. Without a relationship with other members of the *ummah* it can sometimes feel like you are alone and isolated in your beliefs.

A sense of community and mutual support are heavily encouraged in Islam, as it is the duty of all Muslims to build one another up and to reinforce our faith through words, actions, and remembrance of Allah.

Find those brothers and sisters near you, get their information and stay in touch. Meet regularly, work together on something, and spend time with one another. Ask questions and seek guidance for the things you are unclear about. The more active you are in the community, the easier it will be to acquire knowledge and affect change in yourself and even others!

Talking to family

For a lot of reverts, there comes the question of when and how to tell family members that we have converted. In the West, it is most likely we were either raised in Christian homes or secular homes. Islam has a reputation in Western countries, and it will often precede whatever you reveal to them.

If you feel like revealing this information will be detrimental to your physical or mental health, you are under no compulsion to tell them. Granted, sometimes it can be difficult to hide any changes you may undergo. When it comes down to it, the best advice I can offer is to obscure the truth but do not lie.

Find allies among your family members, build a rapport with them about your faith, and instruct them on the fundamentals of what you believe. If you build this relationship with understanding and supportive family, it will be easier to reveal it to the more sensitive among them.

Respecting and honoring parents

This is one of the biggest parts of Islam that new reverts should take to heart. Honestly, it should be closer to the beginning of the book, but here we are!

It's easy to quote the Qur'an directly for orders to honor our parents. However, I think the most heart-felt argument for this actually comes from the *hadith*s and the stories of the Sahaba.

> "[A person once approached the Messenger of Allah (peace be upon him and his family) and said: 'I have an old father and mother, who due to their attachment towards me, are not keen for me to go to Jihad.']
>
> [Hearing this], the Noble Prophet (peace be upon him and his family) said: '(If such is the case then) Stay with your parents for, by the One in whose control lies my soul, their attachment of one day and one night to you is better than one year of Jihad.'"

> Biharul Anwar, Volume 74, Page 82

In another *hadith*, it is narrated:

> "Allah's Messenger (ﷺ) mentioned the greatest sins or he was asked about the greatest sins. He said, 'To join partners in worship with Allah; to kill a soul which Allah has forbidden to kill; and to be undutiful or unkind to one's parents.'"

> Al-Bukhari, 5977

These are beautiful *hadith*s in that they elevate the status of parents to a high place. Above all things, service and kindness to parents is the key to learning patience, humility, and generosity.

Even those pagan parents that did not accept the early Muslims, the Prophet ﷺ advised his companions that they should still honor and be kind to them. If those early Muslims can adopt this kind of mercy and kindness, it should fall upon us as well.

One of the most notable examples of this was the companion Abu Hurairah (ﷺ) who was a companion of the Prophet ﷺ.

Abu Hurairah had come to Medina from Yemen with his mother, in hopes of joining the Prophet ﷺ and becoming one of his companions. His mother, still a polytheist, rejected Islam and spoke ill of the Prophet ﷺ. Saddened by the conflict between wanting to service his mother as well as the Prophet ﷺ, he visited him in hopes to achieve some guidance.

Rather than getting upset that Abu Hurairah's mother was slandering him, he simply made *du'a* for her that she be more inclined towards Islam. When Abu Hurairah went home, his mother had made *ghusl* and professed her faith for Islam. From that day onwards, he would visit his mother every day and make *du'a* for her, and she would do the same for him.

This story is meant to show that kindness, patience, and a desire to do well for our parents can influence their opinion of us and their opinions about Islam. By showing your best side to them, showing that Islam has taught you to be respectful and honorable to those who raised you, you are giving them the best invitation to the faith that is possible – that which you can show. Some parents have even converted to Islam after witnessing the positive changes in the lives of their children, and the benefit of those righteous actions cannot be understated.

However, if your parents are abusive

This question comes up a lot when Muslims desire to honor their parents but face abuse at their hands. Islam is very opposed to tolerating oppression of any kind, and the responsibility a parent has for their child is a great one. To again refer to Abu Hurairah, he narrated:

> "Abu Huraira reported that a person said: 'Allah's Messenger, I have relatives with whom I try to have close relationship, but they sever (this relation). I treat them well, but they treat me ill. I am sweet to them, but they are harsh towards me.' Upon this he (the Holy Prophet) said: 'If it is so as you say, then you in fact throw hot ashes (upon their faces) (i.e. you embarrass them by being righteous) and there would always remain with you on behalf of Allah (an Angel to support you) who would keep you dominant over them so long as you adhere to this (path of righteousness).'"

Muslim, 2558

And again:

> "Abu Huraira reported that al-Aqra' b. Habis saw Allah's Apostle (ﷺ) kissing Hasan. He said: 'I have ten children, but I have never kissed any one of them,' whereupon Allah's Messenger (ﷺ) said: 'He who does not show mercy (towards his children), no mercy would be shown to him.'"

Muslim, 2318a

As Muslims we are to do righteous deeds even in the face of hardship, but we are not expected to willingly submit ourselves to oppressive behavior.

If this means respecting our parents from a distance, then that should be what we do. Have kind words for them, make efforts to establish a connection, but do not put yourself in danger if there is a risk of them causing harm.

Cultivate your charity

Charity is one of those often misunderstood actions. It doesn't mean adding on that extra $1 for Cancer Research at the grocery checkout, and it doesn't mean dropping a few dollars in a beggar's cup. These are forms of charity, sure, but it's as much a lifestyle as it is an action.

Cultivating charity means doing your best to affect change where you see injustice. It means donating your time, your resources, or your labor to help those in need. It means if you are in a position of surplus or wealth, whether with money or ability, to give some of that to those who do not.

Part of what makes this attainable is the *Zakat*, since it is an obligation. Likewise, if you have little, do not put yourself in a position of hardship to become like those in need. This is why *Zakat* has a baseline minimum wealth requirement before it is obligatory to donate your funds – to preserve those who already are most vulnerable.

View the people around you as your own brothers or sisters, as we are all equal in Allah's eyes. Part of developing your *iman*, or faith, is also developing the sense that we owe this world our best effort for improvement. What better way to embrace the calling of Allah to spread the message and mercy of Islam than by lessening the suffering of others and creating a better life for them than when we first came into this world?

Conclusion

It was a pleasure having the chance to impart what little I've learned since reverting to Islam to others. While still young in the *deen* I am incredibly enthusiastic and hopeful that anyone who picks up this book and reads it, front to back, will feel more comfortable with their beliefs and more aware that Islam is an ocean both vast and deep.

We are here to remember Allah, to worship Him alone, and we best serve this purpose by exemplifying that which He has prescribed for us. Our deeds, our speech, our lives, should radiate a message of compassion, mercy, morality, and love for one another.

If you learn to remember Allah and to do good deeds in His name; if you remember to call out injustice and seek to right wrongs in His name; if you remember to be kind and generous to your family and your neighbors, then you are succeeding.

Jazakallahu kayran, assalamu alaykum wa rahmetullahi wa barakatuh. May Allah reward you with goodness, and may the peace, mercy, and blessings of Allah be upon you.

Notes

1. "Fiqh-us-*Sunnah*, Volume 1: Obligatory acts of prayer - Islamicstudies.info." Accessed August 26, 2019. http://www.islamicstudies.info/subjects/fiqh/fiqh_us_*sunnah*/fus1_09.html.

2. "The Biography of Abu Bakr As-Siddeeq - Internet Archive." Accessed September 15, 2019. https://archive.org/stream/TheBiographyOfAbuBakrAsSiddeeq/TheBiographyOfAbuBakrAs-siddeeq.

3. "Conditions of Handling Quran." Accessed September 15, 2019. http://www.*sunnah*.org/sources/ulumquran/conditions_of_handling_quran.htm.

4. The phrase "Radeyallahu Anhu," which means "May Allah be pleased with him" and used for the companions of the Prophet.